BrOken PromiSes

WORD DO HURT

Broken Promises
WORD DO HURT

Donnette Robinson

Dedication

In loving memory of

Vileaner Gamble, 2015 (aunt)

Catherine "Cat" Ham, 2016 (cousin)

James E. Robinson Sr., 2017 (uncle)

Your lives touched our family in such a significant way. You will forever be remembered.

Acknowledgements

The completion of this book could not have been possible without inspiration from God, the true Author and Finisher of my life. Every day since I started on this journey, God has sent relatives, friends, and acquaintances in my life to encourage me, challenge me, and push me to the finish line. I appreciate each one of you.

To my sister, Sharon Connor, who first gave me a word that God was going to use me to write a book, not knowing that becoming an author was a dream of mine. Thank you for that word and for being in my corner.

To my parents, thank you for your many sacrifices.

Contents

Introduction

The world is full of hurting people. Many of their disappointments, hurts, and pains have been inflicted upon them by those whom they love and trust: their mothers, fathers, children, spouses, family members, and friends. Wounds inflicted by words and corresponding actions have broken down their self-esteem, sense of self-worth, and confidence.

When these issues are not addressed, they become deeply rooted in the heart. And once something gets into your heart, it is hard to eradicate it. The heart is fragile, yet it is often the first thing that becomes exposed to the harshness of life. That is why Proverbs 4:23 tells us to guard our heart above all else: it determines the course of our life.

Brokenness does not occur after just one or two encounters with negative words, behaviors, or actions. It comes from repetition: a constant encounter with a person, place, or thing that has brought misery and pain into your life. It is hearing over and over that you are inadequate and you do not measure up. It derives from promises that are broken day after day, month after month, year after and year. It is a systematic destruction of our ability to love and trust.

We get so broken down that we no longer trust God. We start to treat God as if He is a man; putting Him in the same category as mere mortals will detrimentally affect our relationship with God. We stop taking Him at His word. We assume that He will let us down just like the people in our lives have.

God clearly stated in Numbers 23:19 that He is not a man who would lie or repent. He cannot go back on His word. He's the same yesterday, today, and forever, which means He is not fickle in His behavior. All his promises are yes and amen. He will always come through for you! God is ready to heal all your diseases.

Do you think that He cannot do anything about your circumstance and situation? He has the power to make your life better. We do not have to walk around attempting to mend the broken pieces of our lives on our own. God assures us in Psalms 147:3

that He heals the brokenhearted and binds up their wounds.

So how do we begin to look past all these broken promises, and instead live a life of promise?

As you read this book, allow the healing process to begin in your life. Ask God to reveal to you the broken places in your life. Maybe it is hurt, doubt, or a lack of forgiveness. Maybe you feel that no one loves you or no one cares. Whatever it is, God will meet you at your level of expectation. Raise the bar!

Our words have power.
Use yours to speak life!

Chapter 1

How Deep Are Your Roots?

One Sunday during the worship service, my pastor, Zachery Connor, preached an astounding sermon about getting to the root of your life's issues. He read from Luke 17:6: *"The Lord said, if you have faith as a grain of a mustard seed, you might say unto this sycamore tree, be thou plucked up by the root."*

Pastor Connor explained that the roots of a sycamore tree are very deep and difficult to kill. Even when you cut the tree down to the stump, you have not killed the root. He drew parallels between the roots of a sycamore tree and how deeply rooted our issues in life are.

We often cut down the tree of our issues, attempting to eliminate the pain. But just as often, we fail to kill the root. The issue remains deeply buried in our lives. We think the issue is no longer there because we do not have to deal with it.

Then one day, something happens that brings it back to the surface of our life. When it resurfaces, we usually say to ourselves, "I thought this was over!" Or "I thought I dealt with this already." But the truth is you have not dealt with the root of the matter. Many of us repeats bad cycles in our lives due to never eliminating the root cause of our issues.

As I left the service that afternoon, I began to think about my own issues. Why had I associated with women who often disguised jealousy with friendship? Why had I settled in relationships with men who left me feeling empty in the long run? Why do I always date a certain kind of man? Why can I not trust people? These questions deserved answers.

Could the answer to these questions be located at the root of my issues? While talking with my sister one day, a light bulb went off in my head. I suddenly understood why I had not allowed the men in my life to be active participants in the relationship, why I thought it was okay for them to exist, but be missing in action, and why I had repeatedly settled for this kind of relationship.

Most of the guys I had dated were "loosely

locatable." They were around, but not always present. Sometimes I would see them, and sometimes I would not. It was common to see me solo at family functions, parties and other events, even though I was involved with someone. I did not require an escort; I would put it out there, but left it up to them to ask or decide if they wanted to go with me. I did not want to be demanding of them. It may seem backwards, but it was my normal. And it continued to happen because in the end, I knew the relationship was not going to last.

I always felt that I could do whatever I needed to do by myself. I did not need anyone – especially a man. Because I had that attitude, I never raised the bar. I just went with the flow. I could take him or leave him, and usually I ended up leaving. That was my safeguard.

Most of the men I dated were attractive. They were very popular in their sphere of influence. They especially knew a lot of women, which caused me to always be on guard. And whenever I did drop my defenses, the bomb would drop as well. I would find out that they were cheating or that they had some issues that I did not want to deal with. When I confronted them about it, it would turn into an argument. I did not need the drama. This was my singular way of life, because honestly, it had been a part of my heritage for so long.

My mom is a no-nonsense kind of woman who is very independent and strong-willed. My momma doesn't take any mess, and she doesn't wait around for anyone to do anything for her. If you didn't do it when you said you would, the next time you saw her it was done. She was specifically this way when it came to asking a man to do something for her. It is what I grew up with, and it is what I did. She once told me that my grandfather said if you start taking things from a man, they'll think they own you.

To tell the truth, the women in my family are very strong-minded. It is my opinion that most African American women fall under this description. We are very resilient. Our skin becomes toughened by life situations and our emotions hardened by all the hurt and pain and lack of respect and love. However, deep within, we are very tender and caring women; our hard-outer shell often serves as a shield to protect our hearts from further hurt.

The root of my problem was not because I was "Miss Independent". I was just too headstrong for my own good. Looking back, maybe it is possible that I did not allow men to do what they needed to do to feel like a man. WOW! I believe I just had an epiphany.

I think men like having a resourceful woman who will not ask him for every little thing, every single time, but appreciates it when she does. He knows she can take care of herself, but she must be mindful that when she makes him feel needed, it is a compliment that tells him he is appreciated in return.

A curse that most of us feel daily is that we must do things ourselves because otherwise nothing will get done. I do not feel like you should always request men to do things. I think they should take some initiative, but they may not take the initiative if you are always playing both positions.

We all could do a lot of things differently, but we are all locked into our little boxes and locked into our rigid way of doing things. We cannot see outside ourselves, therefore we miss out on what is right in front of us.

We all have hidden issues. People are addicted to drugs, alcohol and pornography. Marriages are failing and leaving behind shattered hearts. Single people dealing with the confusion of a relationship not knowing how to separate love from infatuation, which causes them to act as though a person is their "mate" when they are "just friends." They may be premature acknowledging a person as someone special in their life when it has not been established.

I have been down that road: hearing things like "I love you," "you know I am crazy about you," calling and texting every day, and doing special things together. It looked like a relationship and seemed like a relationship, but it was not a real, God-ordained relationship.

There was always a protective shield around me that kept anyone from getting too close – somewhat like the invisible fences used to keep dogs in the yard. The owner puts a collar on the pet that has an electronic device in it, and if the pet goes too close to the edge of the yard, they get shocked. That was me. I had erected an invisible fence, and anytime I felt I was getting too close I had to find a way to pull back. I was my own electric shock. It is not that I did not want to be in a relationship; it was just that I had been disappointed so many times that I decided it would be better just to not get my hopes up.

In today's relationships, it is okay to be "friends" with many different people and be intimately involved at the same time without any commitment to any individual. There is no commitment: just benefits.

Many think "dating" is the route to marriage, but it is not. Dating means we have something in common and we are getting together to do that thing we have in common. It is not a relationship. Since coming to that revelation, I decided that having someone around is okay when you just want to hang out, go to the movies, or grab dinner. But I realized that I wanted more than that; I wanted someone to share life with. I wanted someone to be there for the important things in life, and to help me make it through tough times.

The problem most of us encounter is that we have accepted the little, supposing that the much would fall into our laps. But it does not. We sit around talking about how we are waiting for "prince charming" or for those who are spiritual, the "Boaz" to their "Ruth." But Ruth was not looking for Boaz. She was working when Boaz noticed her. And she did not sleep with him.

I heard a famous Pastor say that single people need to be out doing things, not just sitting home being bored and waiting for something magical to happen! We should prepare ourselves for that "special person." For someone to be interested in you, you must be interesting. You should set the stage for what you want. You must have some standards. You need to set the bar, then not move it.

In a relationship, both parties should be active participants. They must show up for the good times and the tough times. When it comes time to show up for the life-changing moments, be present – don't just take up space.

I'm reminded of the M&M's Christmas commercial when Santa Claus comes down the chimney and sees the M&M's and they see Santa. They exclaim to one another "He does exist!" before passing out from shock. That's how some of our relationships are being depicted. When you hear the love stories of others, you begin to believe love does exist! The man or woman you have been waiting for does exist. They will even show up in your life bearing gifts, just like Santa! They will sweep you off your feet. They will make you feel butterflies inside. Just make sure they are there when you need them for the important parts of life.

I was afraid to acknowledge the reality of or examine some of my relationships because I was afraid of what was going to happen. I did not know what went on in their life, and I did not want to find out. I was afraid of what might come crawling out from under the rock. Even when I was out on a date, I never felt totally comfortable at times. I guess that is why I entertained at home a lot and drove my own car when I went out on a date. This was my way of controlling the situation; if things went south.

As I think back to my high school days, I see the similarities among the boys I dated. They had the same height, body type, complexion, personality, mannerisms, style, grooming, and love for cars, just to name a few things. Everything had to be top notch. As mentioned earlier they were attractive – at least to me they were. This is the kind of man I have been attracted to all my life.

There may have been one or two who did not fit precisely into that category. They were not as flashy, but for some reason I did not want that. I wanted "Buddy Love," not "Sherman Klump."

Buddy Love and Sherman Klump are characters from the 1996 movie "The Nutty Professor". The movie is about a very kind, sweet, smart yet obese science college Professor named Sherman Klump aka "The Nutty Professor". Sherman invents a weight loss solution and decides to take it after a date with the beautiful Miss. Purty goes badly. Buddy Love is the altered ego that comes as a side effect of the solution. Buddy is slimmer, well-dressed and put-together, good-looking man; absolutely everything you would want – except for his arrogant and obnoxious attitude. Sherman's goal was to alter his outer appearance, but regrettably his personality was negatively altered in the process.

Buddy Love begins to take over Sherman's life and the endearing affection that Miss. Purty once had for Sherman began to fade.

The truth is that the "Sherman Klumps" of the world are the ones who will treat you the way you want and deserve to be treated, but all too often we bypass them for the "status quo" and end up frustrated, alone or both. What was the root cause of this?

Experts say that women usually look for men who are like their fathers. I was around my dad all my life, but I can't say I have an in-depth knowledge of who he is. I have heard that back in the day he was a "ladies' man." I must say that in his youth, he was a very suave and good-looking man. In the town that he lives in, everyone knows him. He is a very popular, influential person. Could it be possible my relationship issues all stemmed from my father?

When I thought about it, each of the men who have been in my life has had some of the same characteristics as my father. The roots of my tree may be connected to the relationship I have with my father.

Growing up, my father was always there. I saw him every day, but he was not actively there all the time. Just like the men in my life, he had his moments. He did show up for the important things: school activities, grade school PTA meetings, prom, and high school graduation. We traveled every so often when I was young, too: Disneyland and trips to Philadelphia to visit family.

Was he active in my life? I guess he was as active in my life as he could be in a physical sense. Did he teach me that a man was to honor and cherish a woman? I do not have a recollection of us ever having that conversation. Did he talk to me about the birds and the bees? I do not recall that conversation either. I do not remember him having "the talk" with any of my boyfriends, or even drilling them about their intentions.

Don't get me wrong: I have a good relationship with my father. As an adult, he and I have had some good conversations and fun; but when I was a young girl, we did not do the things that now seem important to me as a woman. Somehow, I felt I had missed out on the father/daughter stuff and that I had to generate my own methods of deciding if the boy/man was right for me based upon what I thought was the right way.

My way of thinking came from those I spent most of my time with. We all know that our friends are not the best people to take advice from, but friends were all I had. I looked at how they reacted to certain situations and determined whether I would follow suit or make the decision not to be like them; most of the time, I chose not to follow their example or advice.

The television industry often gives a false presentation, a false sense of security, and a false depiction of love and relationships. We get so involved in the lives of those we see on television, especially on soap operas and reality shows. Even though it's scripted, we treat it as if it is real.

Movies and television show two people meeting in a book store or a bar, having a drink or two, then going home together to have sex. Then they instantaneously fall in love, and twenty minutes later they are heading down the aisle to say their "I do's." With these scenarios in your eyes and ears, it is no wonder we have some of the issues that we now deal with as adults.

We have been lied to, but we have believed and acted as if it was the truth. I used to believe that there was one special person in the whole wide world just for me, and based purely on chance we would meet and fall in love. But how could that be when there are more than seven billion people in the world. I believe God presents someone to you, but it is still your choice to choose.

The first time I had sex, I was under the impression that it was going to be the greatest experience of my life. I gave my blessing away to someone who was not worth the time of day. I just did it. I did not love him. I did not really like him either, for that matter, however, I thought he was cute. I happened to be in the wrong place at the wrong time, and it happened. I did not realize how important it was to wait for that special moment to be with your husband. Waiting for that one moment is a blessing.

Dealing with all of this as a young girl was distressing. The feelings of embarrassment I felt convinced me not to go to anyone for words of comfort and love. Not being able to share this with a parent or another adult kept me bound to my mistakes. I remember feeling ashamed afterwards. I was not excited at all. It was devastating. Even as an adult, giving yourself away to a man who is not your husband is not any easier; it does not feel any better, because you still deal with all the emotional stuff that comes afterwards. It just brings a whole set of new issues and problems.

Our parents have issues from their past as well, and children do not come with a how-to guide. My mom was 3 months old when her mother died; she was raised by her maternal grandparents. I do not know much about my father's family or what kind of relationship he had with his parents. I never heard him talk about his father. That could be the reason for his deficiency in parenting skills. I accept that he did what he knew best and forgave for what he didn't know.

A woman needs her father. A part of me would like to say he could have done better, but who was his example? From my father's era, all I can come up with is Ward Cleaver on *Leave it to Beaver*. Ward Cleaver was the picture-perfect father. He seemed to always have a reasonable solution to all of Wally's and Beaver's problems. Maybe that was unattainable. Besides, back then most television shows portrayed two-parent home with mostly white parents. That was not our reality.

Today's example of quality fatherhood is Cliff Huxtable, a fictitious upper-middle-class African

American OB/GYN physician on *The Cosby Show*. He understood what his kids went through and lovingly offered fatherly advice. He was a great provider, a faithful husband, and a hilarious comic. I often wonder what the world would be like if we all had a father like Cliff Huxtable.

Please do not misunderstand the point. My father is not to blame for the choices I made. I am just saying that having daddy issues can cause a lot of unrealized, problems for women and men.

Dealing with these unresolved issues hinders us from living a happy and full life. We allow these things to take root in our lives and grow and grow. Even when we think we have cut down the tree, the roots are still alive because we have not pulled up the stump. The least little thing or situation will cause these issues to start sprouting up again in our lives, and the next thing you know you have watered that tree. It grows back with the leaves of bitterness and branches of un-forgiveness, and broken limbs of trust lie all around the base of our tree. You are left to rake up all the broken promises.

This is what causes chaos at family dinners, Christmas gatherings, or family reunions; we have not killed the root. Family issues are the worst to deal with. Who was the favorite? Who got this? Who got that? Who had to wear whose hand-me-downs? We drag all of this into our adult lives, even though it does not have any major significance.

I was in conversation with someone and he began to

talk about everything that was wrong in his life. He did not have a job, he was in a mentally abusive relationship, he did not have a relationship with his children... he went on about everything. He started comparing his life to those of his siblings, and he felt as though he was not living a life equal to theirs. You could hear the frustration in his voice. There was a sense of urgency in every word he spoke. All his issues seemed to stem from what happened or did not happen to him as a child. Not feeling loved or accepted by his father and being coddled all his life by his mother. The roots of his issues were deep.

How do you talk to someone like that? What can you say to make them realize that they can come out of this and move forward in life?

As I sat and listened, I thought to myself that he needed Jesus. But how could I get him to listen to what I had to say? I could feel the pain and hear the bitterness. He was so broken. He even told me that he did not want to hear about God. He just wanted to be heard.

I let him have his say, then I finally interjected. He first needed to forgive and let go of what could've, should've, and would've been, because holding on to all of this was destroying him. We struggled with this conversation for a while. He was not willing to let go.

I begin to realize that so many promises had been broken in his life. He had broken promises to himself as well, because he would not allow God to redirect his life. The more this person talked, the more he blamed God for allowing these things to happen.

He never took responsibility for the decisions he made that started his life down the road of destruction. He knew the Word, but would not allow it to take root in his heart. He was so caught up in his problems that he could not see the answer that was right in front of him. The very thing that he did not want to hear or talk about contained all the answers.

God is the giver of life, not the destroyer of life. He has a purpose and plan for all our lives (Jer. 29:11), but we must be willing to receive it. To kill the root of bitterness, un-forgiveness and self-destruction, we needed to allow God to come into our life and mend our heart. Then and only then will our lives change through Him.

We determine who we are by what we see in the natural, not by the Spirit which dwells within us, which is who we truly are. We get so caught up in what is going on around us that we forget we are made in God's image and in His likeness. We are more than what we and others see and what we allow.

Over time, I know that God is going to reach that person's heart. I have seen the person change bit by bit and little by little, but he still has not surrendered totally to God. I have encountered several men who have a very hard time being convinced that God can change their situation. My prayer is that every man who reads this book will hear the voice of God speaking to him. They are called to be the head and not the tail, above and not beneath (Deut. 28:13).

God places the man at the head of the family (Eph. 5:23). We need strong, godly men in their rightful places in the Kingdom of God and in the home. Yes, women can raise the family and have been doing it for years in some homes, but it is so much better and makes life a little easier when the men are there to help them. When we all come to know who we are in the Kingdom of God, our natural abilities will tap into our spiritual abilities.

Everyone, young and old, is looking for something greater. We think it can be found in flashy jewelry, designer clothes, luxury cars, elaborate homes, or whatever else that glitters and gleams. I know we have all heard that "everything that glitters is not gold."

This stuff is just a substitute for love or some other issue in our lives. We think if we gain all the material things, we will find happiness. We get all the stuff, only to find that we are still just as miserable as we were before we obtained it. We climb the corporate ladder and find out that success means nothing when we return home to a house full of emptiness.

Some of us marry, have children, and end up divorcing because we have not dealt with our issues. We thought that person we married or cohabitate with would fill the void in our life, but that was not the case. We were looking for love in all the wrong places and in all the wrong faces.

I received the love of my mother unconditionally, but it was the love of the father that I greatly longed for. That is not to say my father did not love me; it was just expressed in a way that did not fill the empty spaces of my heart.

I see little boys struggling to fit in, fighting, getting into trouble because they are so filled with anger and they do not have a father to whom they can go, sit down, and talk with about what is going on in their lives. It's a God-sized void that people are struggling to fill.

I knew a teenage boy who was constantly getting

into trouble. He had been suspended from school on several occasions for fighting. He had a reputation at his school for being a troublemaker. He felt that no one understood him and that no one was on his side; everyone was against him. You couldn't reason with him about anything.

Today that teenage boy is a young adult who has so many issues bottled up inside of him that he needs to release. He feels he does not have anywhere to go so he turned to drugs and women as a way of escape. He cannot go to his parents because their relationship has been destroyed by broken promises. He needs love and he wants and needs to be accepted by his father, but he will not let go of the anger to receive it.

I know men who run from building a relationship with their children – especially their sons – because they did not have that kind of relationship with their father. They use the excuse that they can't get along with the child's mother now, but they got along with her just fine before they had a child.

They cannot communicate with their children because the mother constantly takes the kids' cell phones to intercept the father calls. Ultimately, the father just throws up his hands and calls it quits.

Even though I do not know the whole story, I do feel a father should fight to have a relationship with his children. Both the father and the children are missing out on being a part of each other's life. In some situations, there may be some control issues when children are being withheld from the other parent.

The questions that I raise are: What was going on with them prior to the children being born? Did he or she ever have the thought "I don't want to have a child with this person?" Did they take the time to get to know one another before they entered this situation? Sometimes both parties wish they had never gotten involved with the other. To possibly answer the previous question, it is probable that the relationship was more about sex and less about building a lasting relationship.

The unfortunate outcome of these situations is that the child/children may grow up with all these issues, and the cycle continues, the curse is passed down from generation to generation. We need to choose to deal with it and stop the madness. Just because you cannot have him/her or you are no longer together, do not destroy the relationship with the child/children. You were okay with it when you were sexing. Just let it go! If the marriage didn't work out, just let it go. Learn to give the gift of goodbye.

We all need to have a proper relationship with our natural father, but what makes a difference in our lives is the relationship we have with our Heavenly Father. No matter what we have done, he is always there. He always forgives and loves and is ready to wrap his arms around us and dry our tears. He too bears all our brokenness, hurts, and pains.

God loves us so much that He gave up His Only Son for us (John 3:16). This is the love of our Father. It's unconditional. Even when He knows that we are not going to keep our promises to Him, He keeps His promises to us, never going back on His word. He's not a man that He should lie; neither the son of man that he should repent: hath he said, and shall he not do it? Or hath he spoken, and shall he not make it good (Nm 23:19). The word of God proves that we do not have daddy issues with our Heavenly Father.

Our biological fathers are not perfect. They have made mistakes, and it is not helping our cause to hold onto their broken promises to us. Do not just cut down the tree; pull up the stump and kill the roots. Be forgiving.

Heavenly Father,

I thank you for forgiving me, and it's because you have forgiven me I can forgive. I know that my earthly father has made mistakes; we all have fallen short of your glory. I thank you that you have set me free from the chains of bondage that have been keeping me from moving forward. I pray that as I release all my issues to you, you will heal all my wounds. Just as you did to the fig tree, I pray that you will cause the situations in my life that are not bearing any fruit to shrivel up and die so that my life may be fruitful and I can be all you have called me to be. I thank you and give you all the praise. In Jesus' name, I pray, Amen.

REFLECTIONS:

_____

_____

_____

_____

_____

_____

_____

_____

_____

_____

_____

_____

_____

_____

_____

_____

Chapter 2

The Greatest of These is Love

"I love you." Three words that people long to hear, yet seldom know how to receive. We read in John 3:16 that "God so loved the world that he gave His only begotten Son..." He gave to us what was so dear to Him so that we would not perish, and we rejected it.

We reject the love of God because we do not know how to receive love. Love gives of itself. Love does not take for itself. We give so that we might receive, and we use love as the motivator when it is not love at all. We are so used to the system of exchange that we bargain with love to get what we want. We have done this so much that we do not know the real thing when it is staring us in the face.

As Stevie Wonder sang in a classic arrangement, "these three words sweet and simple, these three words short and kind, these three words always kindles an aching heart to smile inside." The Bible says, "Love cures a multitude of sin" (1Pet. 4:8). Love is intended to heal, not hurt. Love should make you smile not make you cry.

When love is used in vain, it can be hurtful and not mend the heart. Some use love to gain material things only to still be empty inside once their homes, closets, and garages are full of everything they thought they wanted. If we knew the meaning of love, the world would truly be a better place. It is true that "what the world needs now is love... It's the only thing that there is just too little of." (Hal David)

What is love? I once heard an elderly lady describe love as a funny thing. I've often pondered what she meant by that. Could it be that love was funny to her because love can be peculiar? Could it be funny because what love means to me may not be what love means to you?

Today love is too casual. People just roll it off their lips without any thought. I love you, baby. The "baby" makes it sound extra special. When you hear it for the first time from that someone special, you think "Wow, he or she loves me!" It's like a rush. The excitement of hearing those special words causes your heart to race.

When love is mentioned, you begin to get the idea that things are going to the next level. Things are getting serious. Your mind may wonder, what does this mean? Are they saying it from the depths of their heart? Who can say what a person is feeling for another person when he/she says, "I love you?"

I've heard people end their phone conversations with "love you." They said it with no emotion or feeling. Just "LUV YA." It appears it had become a habit, a closing at the end of a call or a period at the end of a sentence. Maybe that is to be expected. I had someone tell me that he just says it because that is what his girlfriend wants; she said it to him so he says it back. Another said if he did not say it, then she would think that he was with someone else and it would create an argument. But what is the point if you do not mean it?

I was often told "I love you" by someone I was dating. To be honest, I did not feel that person was sincere. A few times, it sounded as if it came from the heart, but most of the time I thought it was what he thought I wanted to hear. He explained that this could not have been further from the truth.

He said to me "Just because I do not love you the way you think I should does not mean I do not love you." I responded with, "What's more important: that I accept the love you give me, or that I get the love I desired?" For me, it was important to get what I wanted and not to settle for what was being given to me.

I need a real love, not superficial love. I did not feel

like I was being loved. He was not giving his all in the relationship. He loved me whenever he was getting what he wanted. For me, love was always in question. If you must question if it is love, then maybe it isn't. To me, there was something missing from those three words: "I love you." When love is self-serving, you'll always feel that something is lacking. I think that's why so many men and women jump in and out of relationships and in and out of bed with numerous people. They are in search of something or trying to fill a void in their lives that can only be filled with true love.

I had to learn that love cannot be felt from time. Here's what I mean: no matter how much time you spend with someone, it will not make them love you. Love is by choice; you choose to love. Love is developed over time when both persons are willing to put their all into it.

Most people will tell you that you must first love yourself before you can love anyone else. I would like to add to that that you must also love God. My sister always says that if a person does not love God with all his heart, mind, and strength, then he or she will not love you.

We should seek the greatest love of all. The greatest love of all is the love of God. Yet even knowing this, we keep missing the mark. People are brokenhearted, and in despair because they feel that no one loves them. Not only do they feel as though no one loves them, but some also feel that there is no love to be found.

Women are frustrated that they are not in a loving relationship. They think there are no good men out there. So, some of them settle for being number two because the number one spot has already been taken. To keep from being alone, they would rather be the side chick than wait for the one who will be committed to them and them only.

A lot of women have bought into the lie that there are not any good men out there. If you are an African American woman in the U.S., the imagery being portrayed is that most of the black men are either in jail, dating women of other ethnicities, or in same-sex relationships… in that order. When did we start buying into hopelessness when it comes to finding true love? The world has driven it into our consciousness, and now we have subconsciously taken it as truth.

There are plenty of men out there. I believe the report of the Lord. "He said that if I delight myself in him He would give me the desires of my heart" (Ps. 37:4). Maybe I will have to wait a little longer to get him, but I know when he comes he is going to be worth the wait. He is going to be all that I hoped for and more, because God is not going to give me anything less than his best. So, I am going to wait on the Lord! Single sisters, that was your time to shout Hallelujah right there!! Hallelujah! We should stop this lie, because it is being indoctrinated into the hearts and minds of our young girls and boys.

Women young and old are allowing themselves to

be exploited by boys/men so that they can have a man in their lives. Are we training our girls that having a piece of a man is better than having no man at all? Even if he's a lazy good-for-nothing who is cheating on you, beating you, and disrespecting you, people will tell you it is better to hold on to him cause "ain't no-one else out there."

Some women's only aspiration is to be some man's baby momma, get a house or apartment and let him move in. I think not!

And what about our young men? Are we equipping them to take advantage of young girls because they too believe we should settle for what we can get from them? They are crawling in and out of bed with different girls/women, dropping babies all over the place, and failing to take care of them. What are we doing? Are we that desperate for love? News flash! What we are getting isn't love at all.

I was involved with someone who I thought I was in love with. I believed with every fiber in me that I loved this man. After we had been seeing each other for a while, I thought that no matter what we were going through, love would conquer all in the end. He did the right things, said the right things, and called every day and night. He was doing the things that I needed for him to do, but something just was not right.

But I thought I would make it right. If I would just do what I needed to do (that's coming in the next chapter), he would come to his senses and see that I was a good woman and that I loved him. But that's not what happened. As time went by, I became frustrated, aggravated, and agitated over this relationship. If you know me and you are reading this book, you're probably saying "Surely not her!"

Oh, I knew better, but I was buying into the lie. It's slim pickings out there. And the funny thing was that he almost convinced me to go along with his foolishness, because after all he loved me too. "I love you" just rolled off his lips. But his words and his actions were not lining up with each other.

Love is an action word. Do not just tell me you love me; show me. You should get a clue if you are getting phone calls after dark; late at night, it's not love. If you are just wasting time and not spending quality time, it is not love. When someone loves you, they long to be in your presence.

It is kind of like God. He longs to be in your presence because He loves you. And if we love Him, we should long to be in His presence. You should not have to manipulate anyone into spending time with you. They should want to be with you because they enjoy being with you. That is what it boils down to. We want to spend intimate time with that special someone. We want to share our world with them. We want them to share their world with us. Love is not one-sided. Love should be reciprocated.

1 Corinthians 13:4-7, tells us what love is. This is the kind of love I want to receive, and the kind I

want to give:

> *Love is patient, love is kind. It does not envy, boast, it's not proud. It's not rude or self-seeking. It's not easily angered; it keeps no record of wrong. Love does not delight in evil but rejoices with the truth. It always protects, trust, hopes and perseveres. And now faith, hope and love abide but the greatest of these is love.*

This is the kind of love we should be looking for and the kind of loving we should be giving. True love is all these things, and we should not settle for anything less. If this is not the kind of love you are getting, you may need to reevaluate your relationship with that person. I've decided that this is the kind of love I desire. It is my example. It is

what I look for in a man. The first time I read that

scripture, I was like this is it! If this kind of love is

not displayed, then I do not need it nor do I want it.

Jesus loves, and he would not do anything to hurt

me. He loved me, so He gave His life for me. There

is no greater love.

Heavenly Father,

I thank you for loving me, for being my example of what love is. Because you loved me, you gave me what was dear and precious to you, your Son Jesus. Jesus loved me so, He bore my sins so that I would be able to have life more abundantly. I am thankful that your love never disappoints or shames me, for your love has been poured out in my heart through the Holy Spirit, who has been given to me. I know, understand, recognize, and believe the love you cherish for me. You are love, and your love dwells in me. Therefore, I walk in love. Love gives of itself and asks for nothing in return. Nothing shall separate me from your love. Thank you Lord for loving me! Amen.

REFLECTIONS:

Chapter 3

As We Lay

In John 17:15-16, God's Word tells us that we are in the world but not of the world. So why do we as Christians think that we can still do what the world does and not have to suffer the consequences of our actions?

In Romans 12:1, the Bible declares that "we are to present our bodies a living sacrifice, holy, acceptable to God, which is our reasonable service." So why are we still sleeping with the enemy?

I bet if we took a survey, we would find that there are a lot of single Christians having premarital sex and a lot of married couples having extramarital affairs, but still going to and serving in the church. I was one of those Christians. A saved single, and having sex. I was singing on the praise team and participating in other areas of ministry. I did not see anything wrong with it. Well, that's not totally true. I did see the wrong in what I was doing, but thought I was getting away with it because I was behind closed doors. We figure the pastors and leaders do not know about our private life, so we can straddle the fence. Ponder this thought: the pastors and leaders may not know, but God knows.

One-day God started dealing with me about this. He showed me that I could not be His servant and continue to do the things I was doing – fornicating, drinking, and having lustful desires. Satan had me blinded by lust. I was swayed that I had to keep my man satisfied, because if I did not someone else would; truth is, I wanted sex too.

How could I say I loved God while I laid down with this man? Furthermore, how could I get up and ask the very God that I was cheating on to forgive me? John 14:15 says "If you love me, you will keep my commandments."

I did love God, but not enough to make such a huge sacrifice. That was too much to ask. Did God not know that this was hard? And besides, this is just how it's done today; nobody's waiting for marriage. Day after day and night after night, I would ask forgiveness. Then I would go right back and do it again.

Mister Lover-man was supportive of me giving my

life to Christ because being a good Christian woman meant he did not have to worry about me being a "bad girl" so to speak. He would not have to worry about me going to the club or running up to him at some other ungodly place. The only place I was going was church, work, and back home and that was okay with him.

He would always affirm that he was by my side and supported my decision to maintain abstinence, but he just could not keep his hands off me. He would say he just needed time to change. Making love to me was his way of showing me love. Afterwards, he would hold me as we lay there and say, "It will be alright; don't beat yourself up baby."

After he'd leave, he would call me and ask if I was

okay, even though he knew I was not. And I would say "yes" just so he would leave it alone. I could not even say my prayers before going to bed because I felt so guilty. I would toss and turn all night. The next morning, he would call concerned, asking if I had a good night's rest.

He tried to comfort me by making me feel like we were in it together, but we were not. I knew better. As I heard Michelle McKinney say once at a Singles Conference, "You're cheating on God, and he's watching." That would always come up in my mind.

He did not have a clue of what I was going through emotionally or spiritually. He wasn't saved. He had not asked God to forgive him, and He had not asked Jesus to come into his heart as his Lord and Savior.

But I had. He could not possibly know what I was feeling. He could not know the condemnation, the shame, and the disappointment that I felt. "Enough is enough! It ain't worth it!" I would say to myself... At least until the next time.

I had gotten to a point that I could not sing on Sunday mornings. Physically, I could hit the notes, but I could not minister and there is a very significant difference. I was not singing under the anointing of the Holy Spirit. I was just making a joyful noise.

I would try my best to press through the condemnation and the guilt, but it was so hard. When I was asked to pray, I would pray for forgiveness and disguise it as a part of my prayer for the team when I was actually asking the Lord to forgive me for what I had done the night before hoping that it would clear my conscience so I could do what I needed to do to get me through the Sunday service.

Thoughts would flood my mind: "You're not saved." And don't let it be a Sunday that the Holy Spirit was moving in the church. I would stay out of the way of the Pastor or whoever God was using to speak a prophetic word because I did not want to be called out! It seems funny now, but it wasn't funny then. I was messed up.

The Bible says that "No servant can serve two masters..." (Luke 16:13). We can't have one foot in the world and the other in the kingdom of God. I was trying to play both ends. God knows all things (1 John 3:20); I was not hiding anything from him.

I was giving myself away for thirty minutes of pleasure, if it lasted that long. As we lay, I thought about the long-term price I was paying for a moment of lust. I was choosing my relationship with a mortal man over my relationship with an everlasting God. God is the one who has my back. He is the one who is always there when that man would disappoint me.

I remember crying out to the Lord to help me! I could not do it anymore! I did this a few times until God got tired of playing with me and He said "It's about you; you can resist this temptation. Serve me with your whole heart." I believe at that moment God had taken His hands off the matter. It was at that point I decided within myself that I could do this.

We went several months without having sex. I thought for sure he would have left, but he kept coming around. And though we had not had sex, he was still giving me grief about it. He wasn't giving up without a fight. He still wanted to kiss, and touch. Something was better than nothing in his opinion.

Sometimes we would get so close to the edge that we were ready to fall off, and eventually, fall off we did. And here I go again, starting at ground zero. A righteous man falls seven times and gets back up again (Prov. 24:16), right? That's what I kept telling myself, but I was wearing down quickly. I was tired of falling and getting back up. Sometimes I just wanted to lay there and not get up. I was tired. I could not continue to live this way. Something had to change.

If this man loved and respected me why was he always putting me in this situation? Why was I allowing it? The Bible says, "Submit yourself unto God, resist the devil and he will flee" (James 4:7). The devil was not fleeing because I was not submitting nor resisting. There was such a stronghold in that relationship, and it was sex.

Sex binds you to a person. We spiritually attach ourselves to people we are sexually involved with. We become one with them. Think about it. You have not seen a woman/man in a long time, but the moment you see them all these feeling start to resurface. Not to mention if you hear a song or smell a scent/cologne/perfume, you immediately start to reminisce about certain things. We cannot even begin to know the magnitude of the strength with which sex ties us to people. It creates soul ties.

Now I know why God wanted us to stay virgins before marriage. Once you go there, there is no turning back. The more sexual partners you have or have had, the more souls you have connected to. That is why they say when you have sex with a person you are having sex with everyone they've been with. You connect yourself to those spirits.

God created sexually intimacy for husbands and wives to have pleasure with one another and to be fruitful and multiply (Gen. 1:22). Sex is the very thing that connects a husband to his wife and vice versa. It is the exchange of blood which enters them into covenant with one another. It creates a bond between them that is not supposed to be broken except by death.

God did not intend for sex to be used as loosely as it is today. Because we have entered premarital sex relationships, we go into our marriages with preconceived ideas based upon our sexual history of how we want our sexual relationship with our mate to be. When our mate does not live up to those expectations, we turn to other things or people to fulfill our desires. But thank God for His grace, mercy, and forgiveness. We can go to God and ask Him to forgive us and remove those soul ties from our lives.

Well, the day finally came when I said NO MORE for the last time! I had made up in my mind that for God I live, and for God I die (Rom. 14:8). I said goodbye to Mr. Lover-man. I told the Lord that I was not coming back to Him, repenting again for what I knew was wrong. Being a Christian was more than what I was living. I was cheating myself out of the life God has for me.

It wasn't easy saying "No," but it didn't kill me as I was sure that it would! I had to get used to not talking to him and seeing him daily, therefore I started doing other things with my time. I was at peace. I was not constantly worried about people finding things out. I was not sneaking around. I was free. "Therefore, if the Son sets you free, you shall be free indeed" (John 8:36).

I do not know why we think that we can get saved and STILL hold on to the ways of the world. When we accept Christ into our lives, "we are new creatures; old things have passed away, behold all things are new" (2 Cor. 5:17). I think that we get too comfortable where we are and do not want to let go of what's familiar. We cannot be totally free until we give it all to God. You cannot just give up the easy stuff (whatever that may be for you). You must give up the hard stuff as well; that which cost you something to let go of. It is then, and only then, that God can go to work in your life.

Why do we still do things the world's way? Single Christians cannot date like we dated when we were in the world. We are Christians – "all that is noble, and good, and Christ-like" – so we should be doing things differently, and we should be expecting something different. That something different should be God's best for our lives. Yes, we are still single, but "we are not to be conformed to this world any longer, but be transformed by the renewing of our minds" (Rom. 12:2).

Sex is not the most important thing in a relationship. I think the world has overrated sex. When the thrill is gone, you want to know that person loves *you* – not just your body.

The effects of sex last longer than the ten or fifteen minutes it takes to commit the act. When we become conscious of the fact that God dwells with us and that He is with us all the time, we will stop allowing others to use us outside the realm of God's desired purpose for our lives. I often hear my Pastor say that if your man cannot keep his hands off you, then he does not love you. If he loved you, he would respect you and wait. No ring, NO THING! He must do more than put a ring on it. He must enter a covenant relationship with you and love you like Christ loves the church. Oh, oh!!

Prayer for Holiness

Lord, thank you for being my strength; for in my weakest moments you make me strong. You said in your Word that we are to present our bodies as a living sacrifice, holy and acceptable to you which is our reasonable service. My body is the temple of God. I will not defile it by allowing it to be used for the pleasure of others. I will not allow myself to be tempted by my own sexual desires. I will keep my thoughts on you. Forgive me, Lord! I love you, Lord, and I want to do what is pleasing in your sight. I thank you God for creating in me a clean heart and renewing in me a right spirit. I submit myself to you and resist the desire to fulfill the lust of my flesh. In Jesus' name, Amen!

REFLECTIONS:

Chapter 4

Dead Man Walking

Have you ever felt as though life was passing you by? Does it seem that you are standing still while the world around you is constantly evolving? For a while, all I was doing was going to work, to church, then back home. I remember asking myself "Is this all there is to my life?" Just getting up in the morning fulfilling somebody else's vision, coming home and preparing to do it all over again the next day?

I thought that if I were in a relationship, it would boost my life and give me something to look forward to. I felt I needed to be with someone who could make me feel whole or could fulfill me.

I was in a relationship, but I still felt a void in my life. I complained about the time that was being spent – or the lack thereof – and I hoped that things would change.

Many people are disillusioned, thinking that someone else can make them whole or happy. You make your own happiness. You are whole all by yourself. You must be happy in the skin you're in; no one else can do that for you.

I know many people who have dated, moved in with, and even married people so that they can be "complete," only to find out down the road that they were still discontent with their lives. I have been in conversations with people who were in relationships because they did not want to be alone or were afraid that if they left that person they would not find anyone else. The professionals say that is low self-esteem. We have all been there, however, we must examine ourselves in the mirror and whatever we don't like we've got to face it head on. That's what I had to do.

I was in a situation that was not bad, but it wasn't producing anything Godly in my life. It wasn't adding or taking anything away from me. It was just there. I thought the alternative was a dreadful thing.

We've all heard the saying "I can do bad all by myself." Here's a new twist: solitaire is a one-man game; you don't need a partner to play. I had someone in my life, but they weren't doing anything special. Many of us have been in relationships and/or situations that were not producing positive results in our lives, yet we stayed in that relationship or situation anyway. We know that we need to get out, and we see that it is draining the life out of us, but we just cannot bring ourselves to take that leap of faith.

I consider myself a very strong person and most people who know me would agree. Regrettably, I allowed myself to be in a relationship for years that had me out of character, to say the least. I was not very happy in the relationship, but it was tolerable. I kept expressing my feelings to the person only to have him repeatedly promise me that things were going to change and he was going to do better. But they didn't, and he didn't.

Maybe he tried, but wasn't successful. In all fairness, a person cannot be something that they are not. Nor can they do what's not in their heart. The one thing that I know is that a person will be complying with your request to change. They will change their habits for a little while, until they think they've gotten you off their back, then they'll go right back to their old ways.

I remember making New Year's resolutions that this would be the last year that I would put up with this. I was getting out of the relationship if he didn't do this or that. The years ticked by, and I was still in the same place I was in the year before. I was a dead man (woman) walking. There was no joy in my life. I smiled on the outside, but I wasn't very happy on the inside. I thought I had it under control, but it had taken control.

When you can't be yourself, you are living in a lie. My life had become a big fat lie. I was all boxed in with nowhere to go – or so I thought. No one knew my life was in such disarray because I didn't let it show. And when anyone would ask me how I was doing, I'd just said "I'm okay, everything is good."

When you are unhappy, it shows. I talked a good game, but I had lost my joy. We can sometimes get caught up in a person, a job, or whatever to the point that we allow it to take over our lives. We lose ourselves.

When we make up our minds that we are going to put our all into something, we can lose control of reality. I got caught up in it. I had made up my mind that I was not going to give up. I was not a stalker. I just felt that this person had the potential to be an ideal mate. They just needed some small alterations. They looked the part physically. They had almost everything that I wrote down on my wish list – you know, the one that singles are told to write so we would know Mr. Right/Miss Right when they came along, only to be told later that the list was too long and we should shorten it and be more realistic.

I had lost sight of what mattered. God began to show me that sometimes what we think is good for us may turn out not to be so good in the long run. What's good is not always Godly.

We want things that we think are going to take us to that fairy-tale place, but it does not always meet the qualifications that count for the long haul. We need to look within. We need to stop paying attention to what we see on the outside and what society tells us is important, the car, the job, the beauty, or the money, because all that can change and leave you with nothing.

When all the worldly fulfillment fails you, the only one you can turn to is God. If you do not have a relationship with him, you are walking the green mile to your demise. "DEAD MAN WALKING!!! DEAD MAN WALKING!!" You are dead because you are not living up to your God potential.

God has a plan for our lives, and when we allow our relationship with people or our obsession with things to take precedence over our relationship with

Him, we merely exist and not living. We are dead, and life ceases to exist. We are six feet above ground, but living and acting as though we are six feet under.

For years, I allowed a relationship near and dear to my heart to take precedence over my relationship with God, and I was unhappy because of it. The Bible says, "we cannot serve two masters: for either he will hate the one, and love the other; or else we will hold to the one, and despise the other." (Matt. 6:24). I was trying to divide my time between the two, and it was not always fifty-fifty.

God let me have it my way, but my way wasn't working. I had some days when all was good. Those were the days when everything was the way it was supposed to be, in my mind anyway. But it never lasted long, and frankly I got tired of being on an emotional roller coaster.

When you have a calling for your life, you cannot settle for mediocrity and you cannot settle for less than who you are. You are a child of God. Anything that is not His best is not going to satisfy you because you know that there is more and you are living beneath your Kingdom citizenship.

How could I say that I loved the Lord and that I was His servant and continue to live like this? With my mouth, I had confessed Him as Savior, but I had not allowed Him to be Lord over my life. I had not died to self and allowed Jesus to be Lord, which meant that He owned me – not my flesh, not my desires, not my man, not my job, not my earthly possessions.

It is time for you to let go of anything that is hindering your walk with God. This includes sex, drugs, pornography, lying, cheating, gossiping, whatever it is. You must shake yourself loose from it. Is it adding to your quality of life? Is it bringing blessings or curses into your life? We must take our focus off ourselves and put it back on God. If you hold onto that situation, you'll be a dead man walking.

We're living in the natural, going through the motions but never reaping the benefits of a truly rich life of abundant living. If you play with fire, you are going to get burnt. The only fire you want is the fire of God. It is eternal. Choose this day whom you will serve (Josh. 24:15). I decided that it was all or nothing. If God promised me life and that I could live it more abundantly, than that's what I wanted (John 10:10).

I came to my day of reckoning. No more playing around. "All to Jesus I surrender!" Was my cry. In Mark 10:29-30, Peter said that they had left all behind to follow Jesus. Jesus said that there is no one who has left his house, brothers, sisters, fathers, mothers, wife, children, or property for the love of me, to tell others the good news who won't be given back a hundred times over all that he sacrificed. So, don't be afraid to let go and let God have His way.

Everything you are giving up will be given back to you a hundred times better than it was before. When you begin to delight yourself in the Lord, He will give you the desires of your heart (Ps. 37:4).

You will not settle for less, you will not need to be where you don't fit in, and you will begin to have confidence in knowing who you are in Jesus. This is where it all begins. Knowing who God says you are will keep you from positioning yourself in an ungodly situation or relationship. You will have the confidence that you do not need anyone or anything other than God to feel complete. You will begin to find your true self. You must know who you are, because if you don't, someone else will tell you. Start living the God kind of life today.

Heavenly Father,

I thank you for stirring up my spirit, for letting me know that I am whole. I don't need anyone to validate me. I don't need to stay in any relationship or situation that is not adding to the quality of my life, especially if it's hindering me from having a closer relationship with you. I am made in your image and likeness. You called me into existence and breathed life into me. I have your DNA dwelling inside of me. You complete me. Just like in Ezekiel 37, I prophesy over my life that "I SHALL LIVE!" In Jesus' name, Amen!

REFLECTIONS:

Chapter 5

Who Am I?

What I have written in this book does not begin to even scratch the surface of the many things that I dealt with in my life or that you may be dealing with daily: things that have happened in our lives that have caused us to be disappointed, untrusting, and insecure. I believe that this is what God has given me to write about so that people can recognize the diseases in their lives and start the healing process.

No matter what anyone says about you, you are fearfully and wonderfully made by God (Ps. 139:14). In knowing this, you must understand that it is not what they say; it is what you believe about yourself. The one thing that sums this up is that you must know who you are in Christ; then, the power of people's negative words will have less of an effect on you.

God created man in his image and in His likeness (Gen. 1:26). Then after forming him, He breathed life into him. The very air we breathe is the breath of God. After giving man life, God gave man dominion (authority) over everything in the earth. Then He commanded man to subdue the earth (Gen. 1:28). Subdue is a military term that means "to take under control." We have the power inside of us to cause things to be under our control. Many of us have yet to have the revelation of that power. Therefore, we do not use it, and we do not use it because we do not know who we are.

We are living life far beneath what God intended for us to live. We are accepting the minimum when we could be living life to the maximum. God said that He would even exceed (Eph. 3:20) that if we trust him and follow His directions (Prov. 3:5-6).

The reason we live low-level lives is because of fear (false evidence appearing real). The enemy causes fear to settle in our minds so we do not realize the greatness that dwells within us. The enemy will have you to believe that your greatness depends upon whether you grew up on the "right side of the tracks," or have the right skin color, financial status, or education. His main goal is to stop you from fulfilling your purpose.

You need to stop devaluing yourself based on

yesterday's failures and the negative words of others. You are not what people see or what they say, especially if what they say is negative. When God created you, He created the best. There is no one else in this world like you. God put His unique stamp on you. Your very fingerprint is like no one else's. Even your hair follicles are like no other. That is so awesome! We are more than flesh and blood. We are the very essence of God.

Do you know who you are? You are the body of Christ: His hands, His feet, His mouth. He created you to touch the very lives of those you encounter.

You are spirit. God thought of you in the spirit before he called you forth in the natural. He said in Jeremiah 1:5 "I knew you before you were formed in our mother's womb and I predestined you for greatness." He set you aside for an appointed time to be used for His glory. Do you know who you are?

We can do nothing in and of ourselves (John 5:30). It is God who gives us the ability to do great and mighty things. It is in Him we live, move, and have our being (Acts 17:28). I know there are people in the world who think that they wake themselves up every day and that everything that they have obtained is based upon their own ability and strength.

Some even think that their education has gotten them to where they are today. It is God who gave them that gift. He placed it in them to be used for the Kingdom of God, and they choose to use it for the world. If they knew who they were and used their gifts to further the kingdom of God, that would be awesome. Sadly, they do all these wonderful things: give to charity and help those less fortunate, but lest they start doing all these things for God, their work is in vain. Their name may be great in the world, but it's not great in the kingdom of God. Greater is He that is in me than he that is in the world (1 John 4:4).

The Kingdom of God is at hand, and God is trying to show forth His glory in the world. He wants to use you to bring it to pass. So many people are searching for more when more is already within them. All they need to do is tap into it. That more is the God in you. What's the point of having God in you and not getting godly results?

It's like being an awesome athlete and sensing that you can do it, but not getting off the bench and going to get in the game. Many Christians are sitting in the pews sucking up the Word of God, but not operating in the power of God. They can quote Genesis to Revelation, but have no manifestation. To have the manifestation of God, you must get the revelation of who you are.

Will the real you please stand up?

You are a spirit, that has a soul (your mind, will and intellect) AND lives in a body. Not the other way around. Your body will pass away, but your spirit will live forever. From the dirt, we came (Gen 2:7) and to the dirt we will return (Gen 3:19). Sadly, most of us will go to our graves full of potential and purpose, never tapping into the God potential that lives within us.

God dwells within us. Everywhere we go, we take him with us. There's no reason for us to be living the way we are living: sick, broke, busted and disgusted. There's a seed of godliness in you waiting to grow. It's God's will that we live the Kingdom life, living life by His government that he has established for His Kingdom citizens. Not the kingdom-less life (living by the world's system and its way of doing things).

Jesus is the King of Kings and the Lord of Lords. We are the little kings and the little lords of the earth, therefore we inherit the kingdom by default as followers of Christ. That's good news to me.

Do you know who you are now? You are the child of God; besides Him there is no other. I don't care what anyone else tells you. Our God is an awesome God! If you are reading this book and you have not received Jesus Christ as your personal Lord and Savior, say this simple prayer:

Heavenly Father,

I confess that Jesus is Lord. I believe that Jesus died on the cross for my sins and He rose from the grave so that I might be saved and have eternal life. Jesus, forgive me for living my life my way. I receive you now as my Lord (the head of my life) and my Savior. Thank you for saving me and making me whole. In Jesus Name, Amen!!!

REFLECTIONS:

Chapter 6

The Power of Your Words

In the beginning, God created the heavens and the earth. The earth was formless and void... then God said, "LET THERE BE!" And it was whatever God spoke it to be (Genesis 1). God formed the worlds with the power of His words (Heb. 11:3).

The words that come out of our mouths are more than just sound. Our words have power! Power to destroy and the power to build. Power to invoke hatred and violence and power to invoke love and peace. Death and life are in the power of the tongue: and they that love it shall eat the fruit thereof. (Prov. 18:21)

You can destroy a person's spirit with the power of your words. Are you using your words to build people up or to destroy them? Are your words filled with blessing or bitterness, complaining or compliments? Our words have the power to help or to hinder. The right or wrong words at the right or wrong time can change the course of a person's day and their life. What we say to people makes a lasting impression.

Our words are so important that in Matthew 12:36 Jesus tells us that we will give an account for every idle word spoken. The word idle in the Greek means careless, inactive, or unprofitable words. In verse 37, it goes on to tell us "for by your words you will be acquitted, and by your words we will be condemned."

Our words are so important that even in the day of judgement we will be measured by them. Scary thought, huh? What have you been saying?

Negative words are unprofitable to you and to the person you are speaking to or about. When we say things about people or to them about their physical features or shortcomings, the impact of the words can build issues that are detrimental to that person.

Broken promises can be verbal and non-verbal. Everyone has an expectation of how they think things should go. We expect our parents to love and care for us, though sometimes that's not what happens. We expect relationships to last forever, but sometimes they don't. We expect family and friends to be there for us, but sometimes they leave us hanging. We expect loyalty and honestly, but we are sometimes betrayed and lied to.

Life is full of ups and downs. Take the negativity in your life and turn it into a positive. Be careful of the seeds you plant with your words. Don't make promises you cannot keep. The things we do and say may not be intentionally meant to inflict pain, but it has the potential to hurt others just the same. Speak life to those in your sphere of influence. Use your words to edify, not to curse!

OUR WORDS HAVE POWER!

Dear Brothers & Sisters,

I PRAY THAT THIS BOOK HAS INSPIRED YOU TO SEEK TO KNOW WHO GOD IS AND WHO HE SAYS YOU ARE IN HIM. BEING A CHRISTIAN IS MORE THAN A RELIGION. IT'S A LIFESTYLE. WE ARE THE JESUS THAT OTHERS SEE. WE ARE HIS REPRESENTATIVES IN THE EARTH. REMEMBER, GOD DWELLS WITHIN YOU. EVERYWHERE YOU GO AND IN EVERYTHING YOU DO, YOU TAKE GOD WITH YOU.

Peace and Blessings,

Donnette Robinson

About the Author

 Donnette Robinson is a native of Greenville, SC. She is a licensed minister and Praise and Worship leader at Dominion World Ministries in Greenville SC. Donnette pens her life experiences and testimonies to help others know that they too can be an overcomer, and to encourage her readers that as they press forward and change their lives for the better they can live the Kingdom life God has called for them to live.

Made in the USA
Middletown, DE
01 February 2022